Lávate
Go Wash Up

por/by Amanda Doering Tourville   ilustrado por/illustrated by Ronnie Rooney

Un agradecimiento especial a nuestros asesores por su experiencia/
Special thanks to our advisers for their expertise:

Nora L. Howley,
M.A. Consultora de Salud Escolar/M.A., School Health Consultant
Silver Spring, Maryland

Terry Flaherty, PhD, Profesor de Inglés/Professor of English
Universidad del Estado de Minnesota, Mankato/Minnesota State University, Mankato

PICTURE WINDOW BOOKS
a capstone imprint

Editor: Christianne Jones
Translation Services: Strictly Spanish
Designer: Tracy Davies
Bilingual Book Designer: Eric Manske
Production Specialist: Sarah Bennett
Art Director: Nathan Gassman
The illustrations in this book were created with ink and watercolor.

Picture Window Books
151 Good Counsel Drive
P.O. Box 669
Mankato, MN 56002-0669
877-845-8392
www.capstonepub.com

All books published by Picture Window Books are manufactured with paper containing at least 10 percent post-consumer waste.

Library of Congress Cataloging-in-Publication Data
Tourville, Amanda Doering, 1980–
  [Go wash up. Spanish & English]
  Lávate = Go wash up / por Amanda Doering Tourville ; ilustrado por Ronnie Rooney.
    p. cm.—(Picture Window bilingüe. Cómo mantenernos saludables = Picture Window bilingual. How to be healthy)
  Summary: "Simple text and bright illustrations describe personal hygiene—in both English and Spanish"—Provided by publisher.
  Includes index.
  ISBN 978-1-4048-6892-2 (library binding)
  1. Hygiene—Juvenile literature. I. Rooney, Ronnie, ill. II. Title: Go wash up.
  RA777.T6818 2012
  613—dc22   2011000814

Printed in the United States of America in North Mankato, Minnesota.
032011   006110CGF11

Keeping your body clean is important. It helps you stay healthy. Washing your body removes dirt and germs that make you sick. There are many ways to keep clean.

Es importante mantener limpio tu cuerpo. Eso te ayuda a estar sano. Al lavarte el cuerpo eliminas la suciedad y los gérmenes que hacen que te enfermes. Hay muchas maneras de mantenerte limpio.

3

Owen washes his hands before he eats.
He washes with soap and warm water.

Owen se lava las manos antes de comer.
Él se las lava con jabón y agua tibia.

Before every meal, wash your hands with soap
and warm water for at least 20 seconds.

Antes de cada comida, lávate las manos con
jabón y agua tibia al menos durante 20 segundos.

5

Owen's dad helps him cut his fingernails.
Owen uses a special brush to clean under his nails.

El papá de Owen lo ayuda a cortarse las uñas. Owen
usa un cepillo especial para limpiar debajo de sus uñas.

Dirt and germs can get under your fingernails. Trimming your nails helps keep them clean.

Suciedad y gérmenes pueden quedarse debajo de tus uñas. Cortarte las uñas ayuda a mantenerlas limpias.

Owen washes his whole body in the bath.
He puts soap on a washcloth and scrubs
from top to bottom.

Owen se lava todo el cuerpo en la bañera.
Él pone jabón en una toallita y se frota desde
la cabeza hasta los pies.

Make sure to wash behind your
ears and under your arms.

Asegúrate de lavarte detrás de
las orejas y debajo de los brazos.

Owen washes his hair with shampoo.

Owen se lava el cabello con champú.

10

He rinses his hair with clean water until all of the shampoo is out.

Él se enjuaga el cabello con agua limpia, hasta que se quita todo el champú.

Everyone's hair is different. You might need to wash your hair every day. You might need to wash your hair only once a week.

Todos tenemos el cabello diferente. Es posible que necesites lavarte el cabello todos los días. Es posible que necesites lavártelo sólo una vez por semana.

11

In the morning, Owen washes his face with soap.

En la mañana, Owen se lava la cara con jabón.

When washing your face, make sure not to get soap in your eyes. Soap will make your eyes sting.

Cuando te laves la cara, asegúrate que el jabón no te entre a los ojos. El jabón te hará arder los ojos.

After washing, he dries his face with a clean towel.

Después de lavarse la cara, él se la seca con una toalla limpia.

Owen brushes his teeth after breakfast.
He brushes for two minutes. Then he flosses.

Owen se cepilla los dientes después de desayunar.
Él se los cepilla durante dos minutos. Después,
usa hilo dental.

Brushing cleans your teeth and makes your breath smell nice. You should brush at least twice a day.

El cepillado te limpia los dientes y hace que tu aliento huela bien. Debes cepillarte los dientes al menos dos veces al día.

Owen puts on clean clothes every day. He wears clean socks, clean underwear, and a clean T-shirt.

16

Owen se pone ropa limpia todos los días. Él se pone calcetines limpios, ropa interior limpia y una camiseta limpia.

Part of keeping clean is wearing clean clothes. Dirty clothes can make your body dirty, too.

Parte de mantenerte limpio es ponerte ropa limpia. La ropa sucia también puede ensuciar tu cuerpo.

17

Achoo! Owen sneezes into a tissue.
Using a tissue when he sneezes keeps
germs from getting on his hands.

¡Achú! Owen estornuda en un pañuelo.
Al usar un pañuelo cuando estornuda, evita
que los gérmenes lleguen a sus manos.

Don't sneeze into your hands. Instead, sneeze into the inside of your elbow if you don't have a tissue.

No estornudes en tus manos. En lugar de eso, estornuda en la parte interna de tu codo si no tienes un pañuelo.

19

Owen brushes his hair every day.
He gets his hair cut every six weeks.

Owen se cepilla el cabello todos los días.
Él se corta el cabello cada seis semanas.

To prevent spreading head lice, do not share combs, brushes, or hats with friends.

Para prevenir la propagación de piojos, no compartas peines, cepillos ni sombreros con tus amigos.

While bathing, make sure to clean between your toes and under your toenails.

Mientras te bañas, asegúrate de limpiarte entre los dedos de los pies y debajo de las uñas.

In the summer, Owen washes his feet after he plays outside. This keeps his feet clean. It also keeps dirt and germs out of his house. Owen keeps clean and stays healthy.

En el verano, Owen se lava los pies después de jugar afuera. Esto mantiene limpios sus pies. Y también evita que los gérmenes y la suciedad entren a su casa. Owen se mantiene limpio y saludable.

Internet Sites

FactHound offers a safe, fun way to find Internet sites related to this book. All of the sites on FactHound have been researched by our staff.

Here's all you do:

Visit *www.facthound.com*

Type in this code: 9781404868922

Super-cool stuff! Check out projects, games and lots more at **www.capstonekids.com**

Sitios de Internet

FactHound brinda una forma segura y divertida de encontrar sitios de Internet relacionados con este libro. Todos los sitios en FactHound han sido investigados por nuestro personal.

Esto es todo lo que tienes que hacer:

Visita *www.facthound.com*

Ingresa este código: 9781404868922

¡Algo súper divertido! Hay proyectos, juegos y mucho más en **www.capstonekids.com**